Seven
Favorite Holiday Duets
With
Santa Claus

Parade of the Wooden Soldiers

Toyland

Santa Claus

We Gather Together

I Wonder As I Wander

Chanukah

Jingle Bells

Arranged by
Geoff Haydon and Jim Lyke

CD Tracks
1, 2, 3
22, 23, 24
43

Parade of the Wooden Soldiers

Secondo

Music by LEON JESSELL
arr. by Geoff Haydon and Jim Lyke

March tempo (♩ = c. 92)

2399

Parade of the Wooden Soldiers

Primo

CD Tracks
1, 2, 3
22, 23, 24
43

Music by LEON JESSELL
arr. by Geoff Haydon and Jim Lyke

March tempo ($\textit{♩} = $ c. 92)

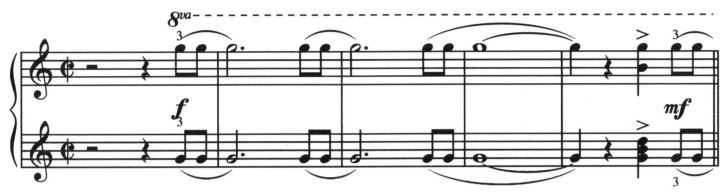

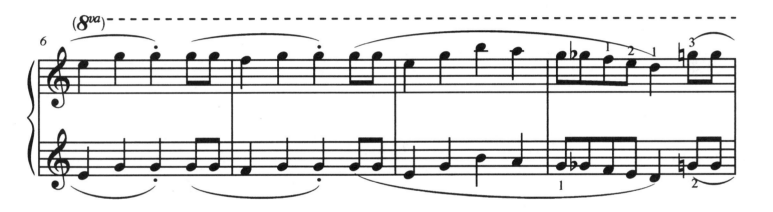

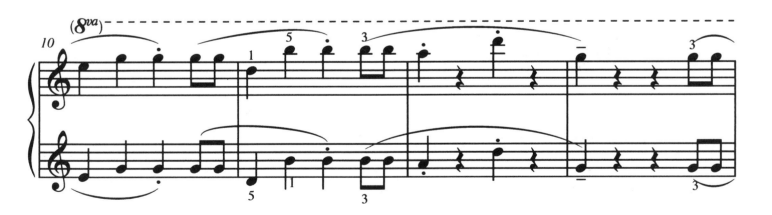

2399

Secondo

Primo

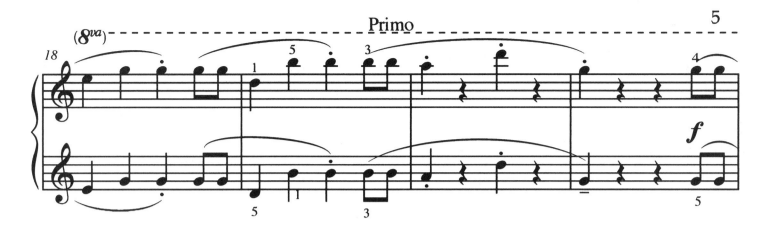

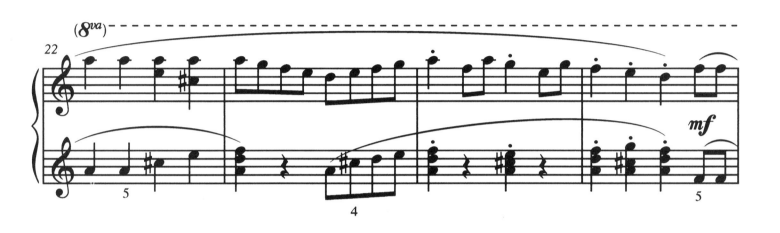

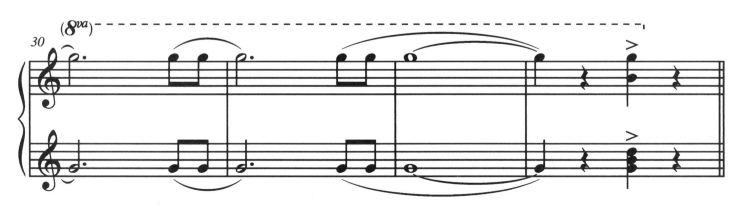

6

Secondo

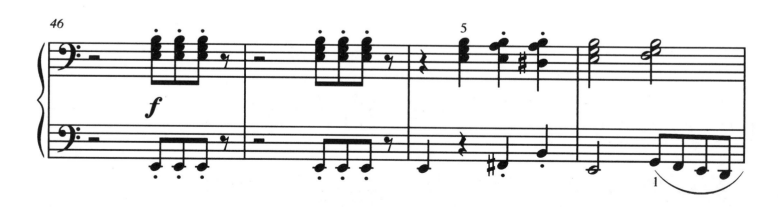

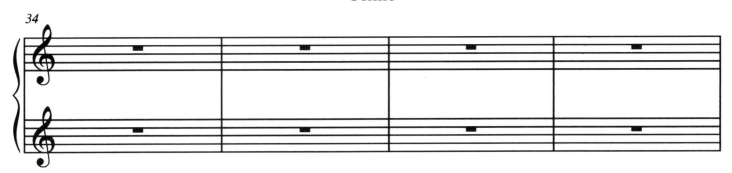

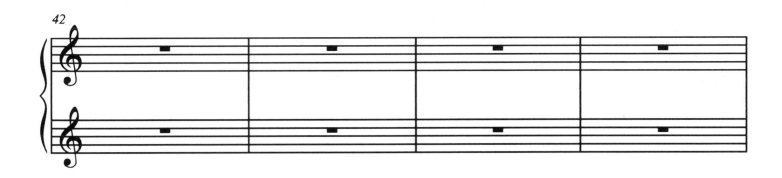

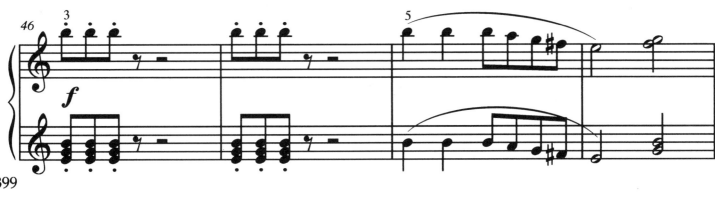

Secondo

Primo

CD Tracks
4, 5, 6
25, 26, 27
44

Toyland

Secondo

Music by Victor Herbert
arr. by Geoff Haydon and Jim Lyke

Moderately (♩. = c. 72)

CD Tracks
4, 5, 6
25, 26, 27
44

Toyland

Primo

Music by Victor Herbert
arr. by Geoff Haydon and Jim Lyke

Moderately (♩. = c. 72)

2399

Santa Claus
Secondo

Music by Irving Berlin
arr. by Geoff Haydon and Jim Lyke

Spirited (M.M. ♩ = c. 72)

2399

CD Tracks
7, 8, 9
28, 29, 30
45

Santa Claus
Primo

Music by Irving Berlin
arr. by Geoff Haydon and Jim Lyke

Spirited (M.M. ♩ = c. 72)

2399

Secondo

Primo

Secondo

We Gather Together

Secondo

Anonymous
arr. Geoff Haydon and Jim Lyke

Moderato (♩ = c. 120)

We Gather Together
Primo

CD Tracks
10, 11, 12
31, 32, 33
46

Anonymous
arr. Geoff Haydon and Jim Lyke

Moderato (♩ = c. 120)

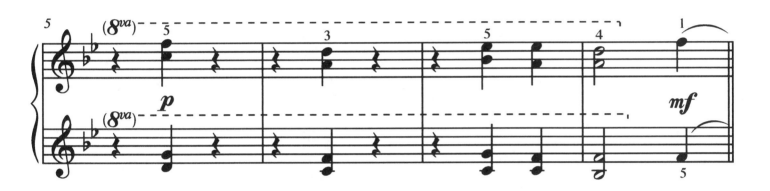

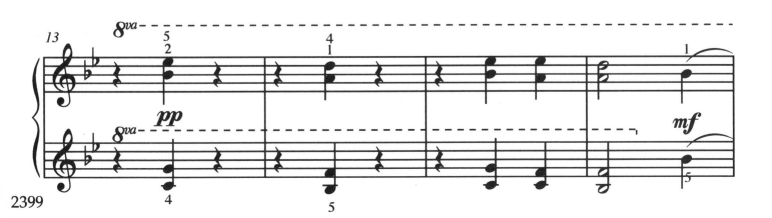

2399

Secondo

I Wonder As I Wander

Secondo

CD Tracks
13, 14, 15
34, 35, 36
47

Appalachian Carol
arr. by Geoff Haydon and Jim Lyke

Slowly with expression (♩ = c. 72)

I Wonder As I Wander

Primo

Appalachian Carol
arr. by Geoff Haydon and Jim Lyke

Slowly with expression (♩ = c. 72)

Secondo

CD Tracks
16, 17, 18
37, 38, 39
48

Chanukah

Secondo

Traditional
arr. by Geoff Haydon and Jim Lyke

Bright (M.M. $\quad$ = c. 100)

CD Tracks
16, 17, 18
37, 38, 39
48

Chanukah

Primo

Traditional
arr. by Geoff Haydon and Jim Lyke

Bright (M.M. ♩ = c. 100)

2399

Jingle Bells

Secondo

Music by James Pierpont

arr. by Geoff Haydon and Jim Lyke

Allegro (M.M. ♩ = c. 120)

CD Tracks
19, 20, 21
40, 41, 42
49

Jingle Bells
Primo

Music by James Pierpont

arr. by Geoff Haydon and Jim Lyke

Allegro (M.M. ♩ = c. 120)

399

Secondo

Complete listing in order of the audio tracks on the CD: